#Broken Hearted Wisdom

M. Bukowska

Copyright

Dedication

Dear Poetry Lovers,

The book you are holding in your hands wouldn't have been possible without a few people, who deserve a thank you. Firstly, I want to thank my mentor, Elizabeth for her practical, gentle yet kick-ass guidance, and rooting for me giving me my confidence back whenever I felt it was slipping away. Enormous thanks and hugs go to my incredible friends, especially Miranda, Rose, Geeta, Stoyana, and Michael for believing in me like only the Soul Family can.

And there's a thank you for those who inspired many of my poems, including My Parents, who allowed me to develop my language skills, and then inspired the Anniversary Poem(#93), a hopeful love poem no less! Thank you, I love you, always.

And last but not least-thank you my Dear Readers, for your encouragement, your 'bugging' me on social media and asking when would I 'publish for real' (well, NOW). Your heartfelt comments and messages telling me how much my poetry meant to you – mean so much to me.

Thank you, enjoy #BrokenHeartedWisdom and come back to it often, and be gentle – you're holding my heart...

~M.B.

And Where Once Was Love…

Demons and Fears are Dancing…

…with Hope

You asked her
to love you
and she did,
How tragic for You
that you didn't know
how to love her back,
For when she'll rise again,
like she always does,
She'll shine even brighter,
but you...
You've lost
The Best
you could ever have in life

Watching the full moon,
Wishing on the falling star,
Waiting for a sign,
A something, anything,
And slowly, realising
That, it is not the stars that are falling,
It is my tears,
It is my heart falling...
Falling,
Breaking,
Dying,
Drowning...
In your silence...

No matter how many times
He tells her
She is the love of his life,
Or how deep the sadness
In their eyes,
No matter how many poems
Tell their story,
Or how many bards
Sing their song,
No matter how many stars
Sprinkle the stardust on them,
How strong his arms
Wrapped around her,
No matter how many times
They'd drift back to those memories,
Or meet in their dreams,
They simply
Weren't. Meant. To. Be...

How come
Your absence
fills up more of me
than your presence
ever did...?

So, tell me...
Why is it,
that even when my Soul
knows better,
my Heart
still breaks...?

It's not when someone leaves you
that you lose them.
It's in that little moment
when you start taking them for granted.

And all those dreams
That fell through...
They were just learning
to fly...

'So, ...where do we go from now?'
He asks.
'We?'
The sadness in her eyes deepens,
'But there's never been "we", after all,
just wishful thinking and maybes,
And "The End"
is the most real thing
we've ever had...'

crushed...
not by
the distance,
the absence,
or the bulldozer
that keeps going
without rest,
but by the echoes
of the sound of silence
from another world,
of things left unsaid...

Enticed by the beauty
of this blizzard
that some call Love
I took your hand
and followed straight into
the eye of that storm...
And emerged
Older,
Wiser,
Stronger,
Alone...

I miss you,
Now more
Out of habit
Than affection,
Every day
You disappear
Bit by bit,
Your smile
Is only
A distant memory,
Your voice
Just the echo
Of unspoken words,
You,
You disappear
Like the watercolours
Casually painted
On the pavement
In the rain...

The saddest things in life
Are not the pieces
Of your broken heart,
But
When there's
Nothing more to feel...
Nothing more to write...

You've spoken to Her
A million times or more,
And you are still surprised
That the stars make Her eyes twinkle,
That She gasps in awe at the rainbows and
fog,
That She giggles and cries
at the most awkward times,
That She believes "The Little Prince" was
real
And the stars still echo with his laughter...
You ask why She turned you down
Why She chose him...
He knows all that,
He knows Her every dream
For, he lives there...
You tell Her that he isn't real
You're right,
He's not,
But...
with your sellotaped smile
the confidence propped by your wallet,
your soul crushed under your mask,
...are you?

A gentleman, in a cafe
Sips his coffee
So matter-of-factly
He seems mesmerised
By the non-movement
Of the hands on his watch
Time
Measured by the empty cups
He doesn't let the waitress
Take away,
By the light changing around him,
(It's almost sunset now),
By the quieting of the traffic outside,
By the couples coming
And leaving ... holding hands,
And he looks at the face
Of his watch
As if he could
summon her face
Into that golden circle...
And then
He hears a gentle voice behind
And lights up
"I'm sorry, sir, we are closing now..."
The lights in his eyes die out
She
is not coming ...

"But... you had stars in your eyes
When we talked last time..."
"Yes... I know...
But ...
I was looking at the Moon,
There were no clouds that night..."

If I could learn
To love you back
It would be easier
And maybe happy
For a while...
Maybe I'd learn
To feel safe in your arms
To dream a dream with you
That we're together,
That our "together" is real,
For a while...
But then,
When life moves in
You'd find out that
I'm really real,
Not your fantasy
That I've got flaws
And faults
I'm not all love and light,
That the darkness
Lives inside
Of my soul
Yes, I know
You want me to be happy
Always...
And you want
To give a chance

For us to be...
And we could,
For a while ...
But I am not convinced,
I don't think
I'm meant to be
One of your fantasies
Chained onto you like a charm
On the bracelet of your life
Because
Always
I'd keep breaking
Free

Yes, I love you,
I will always love you
My heart does not have
The option to un-love
And yes, I am walking away
Because staying
Is not an option, either
In life
There's no option to "undo"...

And so,
You are hiding again,
Behind the verses of poetry,
And, oh, how well versed you are
In the silence
Between two heartbeats,
Between the stars
You are hiding behind the darkness,
Between those casual conversations
And the flat jokes,
That want to be so much more
You are hiding behind your fear
That if you tell her
How you really feel
You'd break the spell
and make her disappear,
or worse,
you two become
...real

Until they meet again,
He will look for her
In every woman's eyes,
He will hear her voice
Whisper his name
In every gust of the wind,
Feel her touch
In every summer breeze
Until they meet again
The raindrops on his lips
Will taste of her tears,
He'll look for her
In every flower garden,
And by the river
they were setting their dreams on the waves,
And every time he'll smell a rose
He'll be lost forever in her scent,
Until they meet again
In another lifetime...
In a kinder world...

Another
"Are you OK?"
Of yours
You keep asking more
The more I ignore
So,
"I'm fine, thanks"
I lie...
For how can I explain
For you to understand
That breaking your heart
Broke mine even more
That I'm NOT fine with letting you go?
But how could I hold on to us
If our dreams dream of different worlds...

It was supposed to be
A happy love story,
And for a moment–it was
For it was enough
Just to be in love
And believe when you said
You loved me
Just a thought of you
Could make my heart skip a beat,
And my eyes would light up the skies,
But in one blue moon
Everything has changed
And now
I want the impossible:
to forget...

It's sad
That you still
Don't understand
That she isn't crying over you,
She's mourning the time she lost
Waiting for you to grow up...

Quietly,
Without ado
She walked away
From the lies,
From the maybes,
From the unanswered questions
She walked away walking tall,
Not looking back
When he called her
And no, it wasn't just a mood...
The bridge between them
Ablaze
And he stared surprised
At the sign on the box in his hands:
"Danger!
In the presence of the Goddess,
Do not play with the matches..."

Long before I saw you
I missed you,
And long before we've met
We knew each other,
Long before we kissed
Our souls already knew
The taste of the sorrow
That our parting would bring...

Like a Waning Moon
That I can
Almost
Touch and hold in my palm,
But only Almost...
You, too,
Keep disappearing
When I'm trying
To reach out ...

And I'll always
Be dreaming of you
I will always
Be wishing for you
I will always
Be longing for you
I will always
Miss you
I will always ...
...give what you can never return
And you always
Will be my greatest
and the most wonderful
What if...

I'm trying to
blow you kisses on the wind,
but don't even know
where to send them ...
Our worlds apart
are getting further away,
and it doesn't matter
where,
if it can't be here,
And I can still wish
that once upon the blue moon...
But I'm too tired to hope,
As I'm closing my eyes,
I know...
neither you
nor the dreams
will be coming...

I'm beginning to wonder
if I'm losing you,
like one can get lost
in a foreign city,
in the fog at night...
But then again,
How could I lose something
that I never had,
that was never really meant
to be mine...?

The moon's rising tonight,
I wanted to make a wish...
But the moon is
...behind bars,
with my caged wishes & dreams,
And I am left
wondering all night
if we were ever
meant to be...

Just Two Strangers
connected by chance,
by the words
that came from one soul
and touched another,
Souls so close,
they can hold
each others' hearts,
feel each others' lips
-if they only close their eyes,
and dream...
So close,
Yet so far,
Universes apart,
They don't know
what they're meant to be...
So they keep on being
Just
Two
Strangers...

not your first thought
nor last,
not even a stray one
on the rainy day
just a random "hi"
when you're bored or low
maybe you'd even ask
why I'm walking away
I'm worth more than that
so much more...

If I were
To follow your lead,
Where would that take us?
And if I were to lead,
Would you truly follow?

When hope is gone
even "Forever and a Day"
has an expiry date...

We both reached
The End
of our comfort zone,
finding the Love so deep
we always hoped and longed for
but never knew
it could exist,
Like the brightest light
we sought
to light up our darkness...
But we've lived
in the darkness too long,
and at the sight of such brightness
our eyes started hurting
So,
scared and brokenhearted,
we looked away
and went back
to the little flames
slowly burning out the candles
our hearts are made of...

Loving you
-the best
and the worst thing
That happened to my Heart

I didn't really leave
You
or walk AWAY from
You,
I just started walking
towards
the Tomorrows
You said you wanted
us to have
Together
Only...
I didn't realise
You couldn't walk
with me,
You needed me
to drag you in,
and I couldn't do
all that heavy lifting
solo...

And Where Once Was
Love...
Demons and Fears are
Dancing...
...with Hope

We were only supposed to
get in touch with our fear,
not to feed it...

The Rivers are flowing
Down the streets
The Angels are folding
Theirs soaked wings
The memories are flooding me,
The memories of Us
Oh how we used to dance
In the rain
Against the odds
And old ladies' envious stares
Oh, how you shielded me
From the storms
And taught me
How to glide on their wrath
Wind in our hair
My hand in yours
The world tearing us apart
Brought us closer still
They laughed at us:
We were too young
To have found true love
Oh, but how we loved
Till death pulled us apart
And maybe if you could have stayed
We'd drift apart anyway
The years have flown
I learnt to love again

But just when it rains,
You come back sometimes
Every raindrop whispers that
You watch over me
Till we meet again
I hope you're at peace

I am afraid,
My darling,
Not that you
Would not love me back,
(that - I could survive...)
But that
I'd lose myself again
If I admit
That I do...

And I have asked
For just so little,
And too much:
A glimmer of Hope
that didn't come...

And there are still
So many scars
That you hide form the world,
And the demons
You're not ready to talk to...
Talk to me instead,
Or the Moon...
I see through your pain,
She listens,
And we both
Understand

Sometimes,
When you can't sleep at night
Because your demons
Are playing with the monsters
under your bed,
Remember they only do so
Because
They are as afraid of your light
As you are afraid of your darkness...
Talk to them,
Share your light and shadows,
Such friendships are so rare...

And all the lies
you've ever weaved
now etched into your face...
And now you wonder
how could they get there
for everyone to see,
you forgot,
that even the ugliest of hearts
still need to breathe...

Sometimes,
No matter how hard you try
to be honest with others,
You can only repeat the lies
You started believing yourself,
And the worst one is
"I'm fine"
said with the most graceful smile
behind which you hide
your worst pain...

Is that what the hell looks like?
I can't remember much now,
I only remember how it feels...
Instead of the light that was promised:
Darkness,
Nightmares
Instead of dreams...
But I can't remember much now...
Impossible to make memories
when one can't breathe...

And so...
I stopped running and busying myself,
and I faced my fears...
they did not run away
they were just there...
clinging to the edge
of an old would,
forgotten but not yet healed,
(well, almost, but not quite...)
Like a little child
clinging to the edge
of the abyss,
hoping someone would come
and save them
from ...themselves,
so they could run again,
-they told me,
they didn't really like being trapped,
in those dark wounds that we hide,
they prefer running free,
running
...to the Light

Sometimes
It takes a lot of Darkness
to be such a Sunshine

But Darkness is never lonely,
It is full of the demons
that come out
and whisper their stories
waiting to be heard,
Full of untold dreams,
Silent hopes,
memories
that want to be set free...

Oh, can't you see
That those dark clouds,
Those demons
That wake you at night,
Those monsters and scars
You are trying to silence and hide,
Are giving your voice
This lovely hue of softness
That I so adore,
And paint that shade of knowing
Into your smile
That made my smile go a little brighter,
And melt the ice around my heart,
When your soul met mine...?

I wish
I could reach out to you
Hold your hand and lead you
out of your darkness
so you could
see the light in you
I wish
you let me speak with your demons
and let me help you tame them
like I tamed mine
I wish ...
But I can't make you
open your heart when I knock
I cannot open your eyes
and see for you
Can't make you see
all the beauty that you are
That we could have been
together
I wish...
and I know
it's just my wishful thinking
So
I wish for
Love
And I wish us
Peace

You call on me to ask
How I am,
And... I'm tired...
Tired of being strong all the time,
Of holding it together
For you,
For everyone else
But not me,
I'm tired
Of vanishing your demons
When my own are waging a war on me,
I'm tired
Of drying everyone else's tears
While mine are flowing into the ocean
inside,
You never saw me cry before
You ask
"Why are you crying my Goddess?"
But it's not tears
It is my humanity sneaking out...

in the shadows
of our smiles
we are hiding
our pain
convincing everyone
but ourselves
that we are ok...
in the shadows
of our pain
we are hiding our fear
of letting go
because you just
don't leave a friend
you love
in the shadows
of our eyes
we hide hope
we never shared
with anyone
in the shadows
of our souls
we are hiding
from the light
in the shadows of darkness
we're just
hiding

Some days
Are too beautifully haunting
To spoil their darkness
With a happy laugh
and dancing in the rain,
So,
I just join in,
Waltzing with the gloom,
After all,
Blue is my favourite colour...

Tonight
My heart doesn't have heartbeats
It's got tears
And one by one,
With my every breath,
They remind me
Of life's every pain...
And tonight
My heart is crying out the oceans
The waves are crashing
On the rocks of my soul,
There's no moon,
No stars,
No promise of the dawn,
And I'm drowning in darkness,
But with my last breaths
I'm still clutching
At the straws of hope...

The Storm around me
mirrors the Tempest within
The raindrops are dancing
with my tears
For once I am not
the Strong One
or the Voice of Reason
or the Bearer of Peace
When no one sees
I can throw around
my own lightnings
of pain
loss
grief...
The thunders murmur
and soothe
The calm around me
mirrors the peace within
"It's only raining"
I say to myself
"I'm not crying"...

It won't be another song,
Heartbreaks
Are too hard for words,
For how can one
Name the pain
That even the tears
Cannot capture...?
How
Can the world still go round,
When even the Moon
Hid her face,
And the heavens are crying?
And nothing can ever
Bring you back
Only the memories are left now
And your unfinished
Autoportrait
And one thing I have learnt:
Death negotiates
with no one...

Darkness...
Such a terrifying prelude
To the black hole of the soul,
And yet,
The only perfect backdrop
That lets the Stars and the Moon
Truly shine

I am writing a requiem
For my demons
All night long
they were dancing with my dreams
Fears and doubts
Turned the dreams into the nightmares
How could I ever fall asleep again
When the darkness
Echoes all around me...

With every sleep
Comes a dream
With every night
Comes a dawn
With every dawn
Comes a sunrise
Within every darkness
Lives the light.

I'm writing a requiem
For my demons.
They were up all night
It's time for them to die

And Where Once Was
Love...
Demons and Fears are
Dancing...
...with Hope

And no matter
How deep the darkness
That you faced last night,
Or with how many demons
You had to dance,
No matter how long
And cold the night,
The light
ALWAYS
Comes back

And at the end,
(Even after the darkest night
It rises again)
HOPE...

How wonderful
And how terrifying
-To be someone's
Everything

When I look into your eyes
I see a multitude of multiverses
And I hope
That in one of them
You love me back

He keeps making up
the reasons to talk to her,
He asks millions
of meaningless questions,
He sends messages
in the middle of the night
saying not to worry,
"it " can wait
He hopes she'd read
between the lines.
The question he never asks lingers...
And she can't help but wonder...
Is he afraid she'd say...
... yes?

It's raining again
And our shadows
dance together on the clouds,
And I'm no longer sure
What was...
What's the memory
And what's the dream,
And it doesn't matter any more,
But when it rains
Like it did that night
I remember again
How it feels
To have Hope...

Yes, heartbreaks are overwhelming
The pain, the loss, the grief
That take up all the space
In your lungs
In your every cell
And yet,
You learn to hope again
When you start loving yourself
More
Than you loved
The illusion of the thing
That broke you

Hope,
the music
our hearts play
between the heartbeats

Yesterday,
And a million other yesterdays
Disappeared at midnight,
When the moon shone
And the stars twinkled
And the lightening skies in the east
Brought a promise
Of a million tomorrows,
And above the horizon
The golden sphere of Hope
Was about to rise...

When you suffer a terrible loss
that shatters your entire being,
and you wish you were dead
instead of going through
the nightmare,
remember that there will be one moment
when you wake up,
and notice that life sucks a little bit less,
that your heart beats a little bit easier,
that breathing doesn't hurt as much
And in that moment you realise
that maybe not tomorrow, but one day soon,
you'll be OK again
And until that day comes,
you'll survive

I stopped counting
How many times my heart stopped
And I died,
For each time
I came back,
And each time
When I woke again and opened my eyes,
There it was,
Peeking at me from beyond the darkness:
Hope...
That this time round
I would not expire
Before I truly lived,
Or loved...

Do you remember
those dark winter days
And the bitter winter nights
That froze your heart?
Nature is perfect...
Some things need to hibernate
To spring to life.
Can't you feel it...?
Spring is coming...

Those make believe rainbows
You drew as a child...
They become real
When you start
Believing

And now it's almost winter,
The days get colder,
The nights are longer,
With every leaf that's fallen
My soul takes on a darker shade...
The nature is slowing down,
And there is nowhere
I can hide
From Hope...

Sometimes
your biggest milestone
is that baby step you took without tripping
over
Keep walking

That quiet revolution,
When You don't fight or scream,
But gently walk away
From the labels
That others stuck on You,
When You leave the drama behind,
And no matter who tries to pull You back,
You walk away,
From them too,
That silent rebellion of Your soul,
When You just let go
Of all that no longer is You,
All that drowns Your soul,
You walk away
From the prescriptiveness of Your society,
From all the should-s, and don't-s...
You just walk away,
And as You start breathing in the freedom,
You just know -
It is safe for You to love Yourself...

The last candle is almost out,
Peace, Faith and Love
Already gone...
And only this faintest flame
Still flickers,
In the midst of this darkness
It still hangs on...
...Hope...

The Voids,
those black holes of the soul
That seem to want
To swallow you whole...
Hang on to those edges
Of your insanity,
The nature abhors vacuum,
Great things are coming...

Snow
In my hair
That's no longer melting,
Times
That will never come back,
The heart
Broken and mended
And broken again,
And mended
And then...
Dreams
That are still in the making,
Life
That will always be mine...
Not much,
But so much
To be grateful for.
And tomorrow–
Tomorrow is
A New Dawn,
Another. Second. Chance.

I'm letting go
of those tiny remains of hurt
from my heart...
They didn't belong there
In the first place...

The footprints
You leave on the sand,
like your pain,
will be washed away
as you carry on walking
through life
into the beauty
of your own
Sunsets...
Knowing,
That no matter
how dark the night,
like the Sun over the sea
You
will always
rise again

With the Sunrise
like the one today,
maybe,
just maybe
I'll remember
how to hope again...

Half moon
Full of hope
For the sweetest
Of all the impossibles

Rain again,
And I fold my umbrella
and turn my face to the clouds
Much to the horrified looks
of people passing by...
But... how can they know
that every raindrop on my skin
reminds me of your kisses
that are yet to happen...

Blue Moon,
Hope
Is rising high tonight...
And "what if"
Is starting to taste
Like "what is"
You
Are set to become
My wildest dream come true...

That part of me
that goes sad
when I know
I can't wave away your pain,
That part of me
that makes me smile
when I think of you,
That part of me
that knows it can't be
but still hopes, and longs,
and wonders "What if..."
That little voice that asks
"Can I dare dream ...?"
That part of me...
It just may be
my broken heart
trying to wake up...

The loves that enrich your life
aren't always meant to be 'the ones'
Or your 'forevers'
But they open you up,
Re-ignite the fire in your soul,
help you reconnect with the best within you,
and if they leave,
they leave you more 'complete'
than you have ever been
Pay attention, smile, and be grateful,
for they indeed, are your
blessings

I give you my heart
And if only broken pieces
Come back to me,
So be it
I'll rearrange them anew
Each time
And will glue them back
With my love,
For I have so much
Of it to give
But now
I am learning
To be discerning
Who can have
a piece of me...

And even as it's falling down
through the clouds
into the sea,
it refuses to die
Unassuming,
noticed by the few,
but still proud,
still there,
almost gone
but still holds on,
Hope...

And all I've ever wanted
was Hope
that somewhere out there
You exist...
And now that I know
That you do,
I want so much more...

And before the darkness comes,
This sky...
The bluest peace and calm
The promise of hope,
And as I look up to drink in,
All is well again...

But sometimes
The Moon and the Sun
Meet in the same sky
For a longer while...
And the day becomes brighter
And the night becomes warmer
And my heart
Starts hoping again...

And when the moon is full,
And the wind howls
Chasing the clouds,
Nostalgia sweeps through me,
The memories are flooding back
That once upon a time
I loved...

...and lost
But with the haunting beauty
Only the darkest night can bring,
I still hope,
I still dream...

My skies...
Full of Sunsets
Full moons
and the silver linings...
And the memories
of you
That are yet to happen

In this disposable world
of hook-ups and throw-aways
His shaking hand
reaching out
for Hers...
Their love
as wrinkled as they are
battered by time
dented by life
Enduring
like their resolve
to stay alive
And just like Her smile
-ethereal
And like the twinkle in His eyes
-eternal
Their Love

(For My Parents ~ Anniversary Poem)

Like the Sun,
My heart is on fire,
Burning bright
As it's dying tonight,
But it feels
The new day is coming...
... tomorrow
And with the new dawn
There will be new hope...

Like the sky
My heart is ablaze,
Unfiltered,
With emotions too deep
To keep hiding,
Soul on fire,
My dreams dancing awake,
And I know
That one day,
Some day soon
You will find me...

Meet the Author

I don't miss
The "Old Me"
I miss the "Me"
I am yet to become...

M.B. 2018

The Masterpiece in progress...

M.B. is a gentle, intuitive, magical being who has written poetry for years
and published it on Instagram...and when countless friends, family
and co-workers encouraged her to publish...she finally did!
She has immense empathy for all of the stages of grief in relationships and her
words will not only touch your heart and evoke a few tears...
they will reach right down and gently touch your soul!

For more info visit: Instagram: #mb_magical_being
https://books2read.com/BrokenHeartedWisdom

And Where Once Was
Love...
Demons and Fears are
Dancing...
...with Hope

Printed in Great Britain
by Amazon